Seasons of the Soul

Pardee Lowe, Jr.

Cover

High above the city of Barcelona rises the Parc Güell, where the architect Antoni Gaudí (1852-1926) built imaginative and visionary structures. One dramatic innovation was his use of brightly colored mosaic tiles decorating the benches, walls, columns, and floors of his ingenious creations. We use a few images of Gaudi's tiles to evoke an impression of the four seasons of the soul. Photographs by Susannah Rose.

"Seasons" icons from the Clipart Collection, located at http://hddfhm.com/images/clipart-free-season-2.png

Published by Quaker Heron Press
5455 Wingborne Court
Columbia, Maryland 21045
http://quakerheronpress.wordpress.com/

PARDEE LOWE, JR.

ad maiorem Dei gloriam

ACKNOWLEDGEMENTS

This book would not have come into being without the encouragement and support of four stalwart friends, Judith Larsen, Isabella Bates, Pearl Seidman, and James Child. Its final form and appearance in print was carefully shepherded by its printer, James Rose, and its editor, Susannah Hills Rose, both of Quaker Heron Press. To them the book owes the pictures of the delightful Gaudi tiles that grace its cover.

To all of the above, my deepest appreciation and gratitude.

Comments are welcome: poems@pardeewaltz.com

CONTENTS

PARDEE LOWE, JR.

PRELUDE

Poetry is
the Divine bared simple,
Life pared to the nub,
and then,
potentiated beyond words.
Poems are the hymns of my Soul!

PREFACE

Mine is a lyric muse
That trips to syllables unsung
And wings its way to ears unknown.

Any season, every season can be the beginning of the Soul's seeking. The birthing of life in Spring, the fullness of life in Summer, the maturation and waning of life in Fall, the dullness and hibernation of life in Winter. Each season brings its own insights, each its own growth.

These poems belie an insight once shared by Douglas Steere: "Before you have had a mystic experience, no words can convey it; afterwards, no words are necessary." Yet those of us whose lives have been so graced often find ourselves struggling to express these experiences, share them, communicate them, however falteringly, in words—if only to others who have also been to the "well of living water." Thus I suspect that the words that follow will resonate primarily with those who somehow share the mystic experience.

Still, I will always wonder when and in what season the spiritual cycle began for each of us? And what form have the seasons of the Soul taken in each of our lives?

PARDEE LOWE, JR.

SPRING

Spring

The bud, the bloom, the full flower glory above the ground. They nourish eye and soul. We joy at the sight of the first crocus, at forsythia in profusion on a hillside, and at fields of daffodils against a deep blue sky. But the real miracle takes place within the bulb, within the seed, within the sprout as it makes its way through earth to air.

The real work is in preparing the soil, in planting the bulb and seed, and in caring for them before any Epiphany. So too with the Soul.

Spring Cleaning

Sweep, sweep
cob-webbed winter
from out the mind.
The dust-bunnies
from your Soul remove.
Your crevice-crannied
being renew.
Now open to the world,
delight in Spring's
each new hue.

Sowing

Root,
dig,
burrow,
bore,
evermore deeply
into the Divine!

Resurrection: An Ant's Eye View

Neath snow-crunch crust
soil-black abuts on beard-husk brown,
clenching angina-tight the tuber's down.
Hard-pressed, long-dormant Bios stirs
with a niggle-nudge and a wriggling squirm.
Upthrust, the stalk butts aside the sod,
all-bud-at-the-burst, craving air and God,
straightway to unfurl its hue—
trumpet-note crisp yellow splayed against the sky!

Oneness

Resurrection is that fire storm of love
that razes the false cities of our Soul,
the desperate longing of the One above
to purge us of dross and make us Whole.
Oneness is the view from on high.
Yet, in this life that breaks apart our being,
that fragments our work, our family, friends,
we flee the One, thinking we embrace the All!

Resurrection Morn

I rise to hymn this resurrection morn
born not alone of His travail two thousand years ago
but too of mine own deaths and dyings now
and of untold resurrections in my soul.

So too I hymn the Light
that blinded those who hastened to the Tomb
and haloes still a Life beyond.

I genuflect the dawn,
the burst of sun on resurrection morn,
and with my soul full hymn that dawn's reality,

for neath its dazzle there bides Glory,

Love outmeasuring mind and man!

Easter Morn

I have no calling but
to hark so deep within
that I imbibe the World of God.

And so this day
I'm drunk
with Easter green,
and crowned
with scent and
hue of daffodil.

His Royal Robe
lavenders my Soul,
and color song
bursts the Tomb.

The Shattered Mind

Resurrection
shatters
the Mind

but
soothes
the Soul.

SUMMER

Summer

Steam is rising from the asphalt, a sure sign that summer is here and that we have de-natured Nature. I spy the steam from my office window. In my mind, I whiff the offal of the chemical plants on the North Jersey swamps, but the name of the sports center, Meadowlands, reminds me of what once was. Heading south across the Delaware, I can now see some Nature, despite the DuPont chemical work's smaze. And by the time I've crossed the Susquehanna, Nature seems to be winning out. Away from the built-up areas, there's land, lots of land. And sometimes starry skies above.

In the summertime, the longing of Spring grows ever stronger, to be one with the All. Can I rise like the steam from the asphalt of my life? From the natural parts of me that I have paved over, that fragment me from the Whole?

Now the steam is nearly evaporated. And the air hangs still. Not heavy. Not freighted with the Past. But pregnant with the Now. Aware of the Future. With the Now, with this instant, with the kairos, that numinous nanosecond which can fuel a lifetime. Won. One. 1...

With Age and Time

With age and time
things taken for granted
turn more precious.

Take the sun.
While I can no longer
walk long distances,
just to see it
out my window—joy.
To sit alone on the balcony—ecstasy!
A breeze conjures delight.
A chair of perfect fit
heightens the experience.
The color of trees and flowers
gladdens the eye.

With age and time
there comes a perfection
to such a summer's day.

Summer Psalms

This is a day
when Sun and Wind and Grass conspire
to mirror Eternity!

   . . .

And so I shall luxuriate in green
'twixt twinkling sun
and sparkling blade,
from grass through grass to grass.
Can a soul so belawned
not but root in Joy?

   . . .

Dusk whispers coolness
honeysuckle hints the air
evening laves the Soul.

A Psalm for All Seasons

I must scale the World down to its true immensities
pare the meaningless pulp of my words to those of pith
and trim my hectic days to hours of transcendent power.

Island

I am sunning in reverie. The lake laps against the island's shore with an irregular music that calms my nerves. Teals swim by, in twos and threes, and even sixes. And I have had only a half dozen days here in paradise. A day-and-a-half business trip has broken a string of halcyon days. But even the day-and-a-half left is better than nothing and is returning me to some composure.

The winter here is bitter cold. So I don't come here then. But the summer and early fall are delightful. A cool breeze tangents my face. And the view of the waves and other islands bespeaks another life, a calmer, more tranquil time. Here the Spirit is palpable. I feel it. I hear it. I smell it in an air that has a clear, clean edge.

I suppose there are those who find the Spirit in the city, a noisy tranquility of a different ilk. Yes, the Spirit is everywhere. Over all. Over every thing, even in town. But it is extraordinary here on the island.

Two years ago I was summoned to be an angel. Not to guide, not to protect, not to save—simply to be there prayerfully for two people I had met here. They don't know it, but they have been the object of that summons ever since. I don't rise or retire with their names on my lips. Rather the Spirit bids me recollect their lives in dart-like calls. Sometimes at moments of deepest personal pain for myself, the summons comes. Friends seem to write little about prayer. Yet, suddenly, here is the Spirit. Here is the call. Begun on the isle, the call returns more forcefully during my non-vacation life. In the pain of life, is it a call to wider awareness, fuller humanity, or a recollection of the Peace of the Isle?

Time and again I wonder if I have a right to deny the summons. Why am I writing about it? What right? Yet, what right have I to say nay when I have been called? And so the Archer of the Lord spans the Bow of the Soul and aims another Arrow Prayer:

Holy Angels, hover round.
Cover air and sea and ground.
Wing where e'er need be found.
Holy Angels, hover round.

FALL

Lead kindly Light,
amid th'-encircling gloom,
Lead thou me on ....

John Henry Newman

Fall

Fall shows a Janus face, the culmination of growth and the dying away of its bearers. The pumpkin ripens, the turkey fattens, Thanksgiving brings a groaning board. We celebrate the harvest's fullness and glory in Fall's colors.

Fanfare

Just over the hill
Fall bursts into view,
prodigal of leaf
spectacular of hue.

The Janus Face of Fall

A majesty of maples crowned the hill below
till their reds and yellows quarreled
with a hint of coming snow.
Now their leaves are drained of orange
and burnt to parchment brown,
and winter's tread falls leaden
'cross the barren ground.

Autumn Twist

Presto:

> Oh the winds
> the winds
> in their technicolor whirl
> of the leaves
> the leaves
> that sail and swirl
> through the sky
> the sky
> gladdening the eye.

Adagio:

> Behold
> how Autumn brightness
> unfurls

Lento:

> unfurls.

Autumn Triptych

Preludio:

> I'm attuned to Fall —
> light and leaves tumble out the heavens
> shattering prisms across the land.

Prestissimo ed adagio:

In the fall at their falling
the leaves leave off leafing
and levitate lithely to the litmus of life.
In the winds they're a-whirling
in wreathes color blinding
dancing a jig on the edge of a knife.
And their veins are bled
from blazing to orange
foretoken of winter's chill...
and ice.

Allegro:

In riot red my autumn'd soul
glories in scent of fall,
in silvery glint of speckled moon,
in crunch of leaf beneath it all,
in whirling, swirling clouds of leaves
that scud and twist about the sky,
in crinkling, crackly orange hues,
whose only recourse is to die.
Say, brittle leaf, there at my feet,
bound soon to expire,
did you spy that seed half-buried there,
ready ev'n now at spring's rebirth to conspire?

On the Cusp

It's a woodwind time of year
Roulades roil the air
The first shrill tones out winter's reed.

Transition

Fall has gloried, and our only near prospect is Winter's gloom. Autumn paradoxes Life! So much of it is beautiful, so much bleak, so much prospect, so much pain. In some languages, like German *der Herbst* and Icelandic *haustið*, the words for Autumn relate to the English "harvest," to the fullness, to the ripeness, to the maturity of Life. In others, like Danish *efteråret* and Dutch *het najaar*, the words refer to the fullness dying away, to its bleakness, to endings!

Only by living do we survive the bleakness, do we learn that Spring follows Winter which, before that, has followed Fall. For those who never live beyond that first remove, Autumn must betoken Death! Yet for the rest of us, there lurks the distant prospect of Spring, known only experimentally, experientially—most especially, in the Spirit.

Beauty and bleakness, pain and prospect—in the Spirit. These are the leaves the Fall wind blows this way.

PARDEE LOWE, JR.

WINTER

Winter

Winter's a time for hunkering down. For getting the inside outside and the outside inside. For gazing at, beholding, and then seeing a veiled world, frozen in beauteous sterility. Or is it? What lurks neath the ice?

Winter's a time to seek deep. Neath the snow. Neath the frozen ground. A time to stumble, slip, and free-fall into the fecundity of the Spirit. Neath the hard, icy crust of a mundane world seethes the magma of God.

In the dull grey doldrum days of winter
where, then, the whisperings of my soul?

Advent

The dark is inching
sure-footed into night
past a tiny spark
that too will grow
imperceptibly
across the days
till at the last
it heralds bright

      the Light of the World

A Modern Magnificat

> *But Mary kept all these things,
> and pondered them in her heart.
> Luke 2:19 KJV*

God is wingèd.

  God is still.

God is the breath …

  in a breeze …

    that never stirs …

      yet whispers eternally through my Soul.

Mary's Song of the Seed

Rise, O Heart,
at the stirring of the Seed.
Feed, O Soul,
its inner need.
And when in fullness
the seedling's grown,
soar in joy
over the Tree.

Silent Night

In the ozone fire-fall of heaven
where meteors splatter 'gainst a palette sky,
out on the ragged edge of nowhere,
midst a black hole's windward eye,
in the fiery tail of the comet,
and the fecund mind of man,

the depths of holy silence splendor,
    the harmonies of God.

Nativity

Black was the Nativity
Till into that dark night
There burst a star,
And God re-liven-ed Man.

Star Song

Late the Star shone on men
Later still it may return.
Yet the Soul retains its gleam,
Hymn, oh Heart, the Gift within!

No Falling Star

T'was no falling star that night
that guided to the Babe.
Wisemen and shepherds were among the few,
and since, too few have aimed their steps
towards Bethlehem.

So kneel at the crib
behold the Child
bethink His natal star
and know it glows in thee.

    Soar, O Heart.
       and hymn the gift within!

Adoration

Wordless, I receive Thee!
Awed, I adore Thee!

Joyous,
    I join in the flow of Thy Love!

PARDEE LOWE, JR.

The Challenge of the Nativity

The challenge of the Babe
lying naked in the manger
   is tendering.

Do you see Him in the homeless man
   curled on the steam vent in the park?
Do you see Him in the baglady
   schlepping her few goods in the grocery cart?
Do you see Him in the kid dealing drugs
   there on the corner?
Do you hear Him in the desperate cries
   of the crack baby in the streetwalker's arms?

Why then did you walk away?

The Gift

In the end, God has no hands but ours.
In the end, Christ becomes in us.
In the end. Light and Love and Mirth shine through us.
        May Joy birth our Nativity!

Midwinter Passion

The babe is the passion of God,
the gift of a sorrowing, caring Father
to His dysfunctional world family,
and the first joyous step
in the rebirth of man
in the image of God.

"What Became of the Star, Daddy?"

"What became of the Star, Daddy?" asked Carol.

"Oh Carol!" snorted her brother, Edward. "That's a dumb question."

"It burned up!" announced Andy, older and wiser in things scientific.

"Yeah, they told us all about it at the planetarium," said Alice. "How it was a comet and drifted away again. Or a super star that burned up. Or three planets getting together once every ... I don't know how many years, like ... uh .... Edward said, 'It's a dumb question!'"

Then Carol wailed: "But what became of the Star? It was so bright and beautiful. And it showed everybody where Jesus lay."

We had just finished the Christmas readings in Luke and Matthew, and of course, *The Littlest Angel*, that story full of truth and beauty, perhaps more meaningful to tender grown-ups than to the young. *The Littlest Angel* has often reduced me to tears (me a 46-year-old male) as The Littlest Angel's gift box with its dog's collar, and butterfly, and other earthly things rises to become the star.

The warmth from the readings lingered as Carol asked once again, "What became of the Star?" Of course, I thought, scientifically, Alice must be right.

Yet out of the glow I sensed that God could create a Star to announce the Savior's coming so he could work another miracle after Jesus' birth.

Suddenly in my mind's eye, I saw what He had done. As men returned to the daily round, the shepherds to their flocks, the visitors from the inn to their home towns, the inn's owner to his daily chores, God took down the Star from the sky saying,

"Some saw the Star's splendor a little while, then turned away. But for those who faithfully followed it or shall come to truly know my Son in the fulness of His Being and Grace, to them I shall give a piece of the Star. It shall warm them in the cold World; whenever the World seems darkest it shall light Life's way.

No more shall men see the Star in the sky. But for those who come to love my Son, it shall glow in their hearts."

And so, throughout the Ages for those who have heard His story and come to adore the Christ, the Star has glowed in their hearts. Friends call it "The Light Within."

"What became of the Star, Daddy?"

"Why, child, it now shines in your heart!"

Modern Epiphany

Were Christ to be born today, into our busy, harried, spiritually unfocused world—to such a world, the Magi might bring three rather different gifts:

A love of Silence,

An ability to Listen, and

A willingness to be led by the Spirit!

PARDEE LOWE, JR.

A Friendly Epiphany

For a month I have been meditating on the Christmas Story. This train of thought was triggered by the reminder that a court order had barred the town of Vienna, Virginia, from displaying a creche on town land. Now, however one may feel about that problem, it raises the very real question of the place of the Christmas Story in a multi-cultural society.

Has the Christmas Story outlived its usefulness? Is its message so freighted with theology that it fails to communicate to people, no matter their race, creed, or religion?

And so I began a month-long meditation on the meaning of the Christmas story. I was led to five thought circles around the story of the Birth. I suspect that the insights I arrived at hold true for the Spirit wherever it is abroad, among whatever people, through whatever religion. But as I live in the western world, my insights often come in western, Christian garb. So this is the form in which I must share them.

The first thought circle relates to the telling of the news. It was to the shepherds and the Wise Men that the news came: to two groups waiting in expectant stillness. Perhaps the shepherds expected no more than to get through the night and to see that their tally at dawn agreed with their count at dusk. But the message came to them. And it came as well to the Wise Men, who were expecting something, and who, in fact, had been hunting for some time. Thus, the first thought is that the Spirit tends to bide with those who practice expectant stillness.

The second thought circle concerns the shepherds' reaction to the news. Certainly, they were blinded by the light, and startled by the message. Yet, when it was all over, they simply accepted it, saying, 'Well, let's go take a look!" So the Spirit seems to come to those who practice simple acceptance.

The third and fourth thought circles involve the Wise Men. They had been searching for a sign for some time. Scanning the night sky, they were diligent in their looking. So the Spirit seems to bide with those who practice whole-hearted seeking.

Moreover, the Wise Men found the sign and were led by it. Initially, the light they saw may have been no more than a pin-prick in the sky. Yet, they honored the leading and followed it to the Babe. It is thought that they were Zoroastrians, from Persia or, perhaps, even the western part of India. In the days of no planes, trains, or cars, they traveled far to follow the star and at great personal sacrifice. And so the Spirit seems to abide with those who honor its leadings.

The fifth thought circle relates to the Birth, to the Babe. We all recognize birth as a kind of miracle and each baby as a new thing. Perhaps at no other time in its life will it have so little material and psychological baggage and such vast possibilities for growth and development. As adults, we even envy a newborn for this. Yet, the other settings in which the Spirit appeared in the story—expectant stillness, simple acceptance, wholehearted seeking, and honoring the Spirit's leadings—suggest that we too can be reborn. And so the Spirit tends to come to those who hallow the child, both the newborn and the reborn.

How striking that the story of the Birth, which begins with two parents seeking a place where their child may be born, contains, in the final analysis, an almost hidden list of five dwelling places of the Spirit—possible places where we may be reborn.

May Joy in the Spirit birth our Nativity!

CHANGING YEARS

The Cycle Ends

So the round of seasons is complete. And it's time to contemplate the change of years. A new year begins—and challenges the spirit—amidst a melancholy of good-byes to the past and a celebration of the future to come.

Into and Out of the Mists on New Year's Eve

Soon memory
will grandfather this year.
And for a while
its peaks and valleys
retain their contours,
but gradually recede
into the mist
of past years.

When at the very end
the mists clear,
what will be
the landscape of my life?

The Past Year

The year is past now
past beyond retrieving
receding hour by hour
into its pastness, past ...
paster ... pastest....

And it recks our deeds.
Could we but alter them,
rerail life—but they are past,
past... paster ... pastest...
in a temporal comparison
that will stretch throughout
our life.

So every year
at its ending falls away to be
forgot or recked as
mind and memory
allow, either to be altered
to our perspective, gentler,
kinder than their reality, or
to be disrobed starkly
in their truth.

PARDEE LOWE, JR.

New Year's Resolution

From the first second after midnight
the year times itself anew
and I resolve to sense all things
more fully, to feel the flow of time
and joy in it. So I shall hark
to the leaf as it greens itself
and to the bud as it flowers.
I shall sense its color, delight
in its very tint and hue. I shall
see the wind both in its fullness
as a gale and in the stillness
of its calm. The ground beneath
me will soothe my feet
with its crunch, and I shall joy
in the stride the path invites.
I shall bask in human kindness
wherever I find it.
I will hear the sun as it beams
its warmth down upon me
and reach out and touch
the surface of the moon.
I will hear the twinkle
of the stars and feel
the patterns of their
constellations, bathe
in the Milky Way, and
touch the tail of a comet.
And while Chronos ticks
away the seconds, minutes,

41

hours, I will sense rather
that time where all things
come into their own, and
cherish those moments
which mirror Eternity.

The New Year Comet

New Year descends upon us
like a comet, its head
the glittering ball in Times Square
with champagne and noisemakers,
even fireworks as its tail.

In a year, when we glance back,
what will have come in its wake?
Will we be different? Will we be here?

PARDEE LOWE, JR.

Ring in the New Year!

In the
beginning
and at the end
it's the simple things.
And in the middle—
well, mid-life is like
a carousel spinning
faster and faster:
get a job,
find a mate
get a raise
have kids
get a better job
buy a bigger house
or is it a bigger car,
or maybe even both,
join the country club,
drive the kids to school,
then to hockey or soccer,
or to riding lessons or ballet,
whatever until you can't turn around
without something urgent needing to be done.
The
real art
is to find
space and time
for the simple things
at the busiest of moments.
In the end, they're really
the only pleasures
that last.

CODA

These poems have spanned a complete cycle of seasons—
so spring is just around the corner again. How differently
the Spirit manifests itself in each season—in the bursting
of spring, the warmth of summer, in the harvest of fall, in
the loss of winter. What then is the thread through them
all? Silence? Change? Transcendence?

The Spirit thrives
in the crevices of our Life
where things don't quite neatly fit
and our wishes don't always work out.

PARDEE LOWE, JR.

Made in the USA
Middletown, DE
24 December 2019